Contents

Breakfast tastes

Toast tastes **delicious** with strawberry jam.

4

What can I...?

Taste

Sue Barraclough

HEINEMANN
LIBRARY

Little Nippers

www.heinemann.co.uk/library
Visit our website to find out more information about **Heinemann Library** books.

To order:
☎ Phone 44 (0) 1865 888066
🖷 Send a fax to 44 (0) 1865 314091
💻 Visit the Heinemann Bookshop at www.heinemann.co.uk/library to browse our catalogue and order online.

First published in Great Britain by Heinemann Library, Halley Court, Jordan Hill, Oxford OX2 8EJ, part of Harcourt Education. Heinemann is a registered trademark of Harcourt Education Ltd.

Editorial: Sarah Shannon and Louise Galpine
Design: Jo Hinton-Malivoire and Tokay, Bicester, UK (www.tokay.co.uk)
Picture Research: Melissa Allison
Production: Camilla Smith

Originated by Chroma Graphics (Overseas) Pte.Ltd.
Printed and bound in China by South China Printing Company

ISBN 0 431 02206 2 (hardback)
ISBN 978 0 431 02206 2 (hardback)
09 08 07 06 05
10 9 8 7 6 5 4 3 2 1

ISBN 0 431 02212 7 (paperback)
ISBN 978 0 431 02212 3 (paperback)
09 08 07
10 9 8 7 6 5 4 3 2

British Library Cataloguing in Publication Data
Barraclough, Sue
What can I? – Taste
612.8'7
A full catalogue record for this book is available from the British Library.

Acknowledgements
The Publishers would like to thank the following for permission to reproduce photographs:
Corbis p.**19** left and right insets; Eyewire p.**11**; Getty Images/PhotoDisc p.**23** top inset; Harcourt Education pp.**6-7**, **12** top inset, **14**(Gareth Boden), **10**, **12** bottom inset, **15** (Trevor Clifford), **4-5**, **8-9**, **16**, **17**, **18**, **19**, **20-21**, **22**(Tudor Photography); Punchstock pp.**12-13**.

Cover photograph reproduced with permission of Harcourt Education Ltd. / Tudor Photography.

Every effort has been made to contact copyright holders of any material reproduced in this book. Any omissions will be rectified in subsequent printings if notice is given to the Publishers.

2

What is your favourite breakfast **taste**?

5

Toothpaste tastes

Toothpaste tastes **fresh** and **clean**.

What does your toothpaste **taste** like?

Minty!

Fizzy!

Shopping

Shopping for food is fun.

Sometimes you can taste things before you buy them.

Fruity tastes

Look at all the different fruit. Can you see the round oranges?

How do lemons **taste**?

Mmmm, ice cream **tingles** on your tongue!

Chocolate

Strawberry

Lemon

Which ice cream would you choose?

11

Picnic tastes

Yum! What would you choose to eat first?

Is there anything you do not want to taste?

Munch!

Crunch!

Preparing food

Preparing party food is **fun**...

Yummy!

Mmmm!

...but **tasting** everything is the best part!

Birthday tastes

What flavour do you think the cake is?

Tasty games

Can you guess what each thing tastes like?

Crisps are... **salty**.

Lemon is... **sour**.

Chocolate is... sweet.

Apples taste **juicy** and sweet.

splash!

Party treats

Everyone takes treats home from a birthday party.

Which party bag would you choose?

sweet

sour

salt

... and finally milky hot chocolate.

Index

Notes for adults

This series encourages children to explore their environment to gain knowledge and understanding of the things they can see, smell, hear, taste, and feel. The following Early Learning Goals are relevant to the series:

• use the senses to explore and learn about the world around them
• respond to experiences and describe, express, and communicate ideas
• make connections between new information and what they already know
• ask questions about why things happen and how things work
• discover their local environment and talk about likes and dislikes.

The following additional information may be of interest
The tongue is covered in small bumps called taste buds. The taste buds are made up of cells that detect flavour. There are four main tastes – sweet, sour, salty, and bitter, and each one is detected on a different area of the tongue.

Follow-up activities
On a trip to the supermarket talk about different tastes, favourite flavours, and foods they wouldn't choose and why. Then encourage children to make drawings and paintings of their favourite foods.